2/16

SURPRISINGLY SCARY!

Look Out for the
RACCOON!

Caitie McAneney

PowerKiDS
press.

New York

Published in 2016 by The Rosen Publishing Group, Inc.
29 East 21st Street, New York, NY 10010

First Edition

Editor: Caitlin McAneney
Book Design: Katelyn Heinle

Photo Credits: Cover Tom Reichner/Shutterstock.com; back cover, pp. 3, 4, 6, 8, 10, 12, 14, 16, 18, 20, 22–24 (background) CAMPINCOOL/Shutterstock.com; p. 4 James Coleman/Shutterstock.com; p. 5 Phil Lowe/Shutterstock.com; p. 7 (raccoon) mb-fotos/Thinkstock.com; p. 7 (map inset) ekler/Shutterstock.com; p. 9 John Pitcher/Thinkstock.com; p. 10 Meinzahn/Thinkstock.com; p. 11 Kletr/Shutterstock.com; p. 12 Colette3/Shutterstock.com; p. 13 Becky Sheridan/Shutterstock.com; p. 15 vm/Shutterstock.com; p. 16 Horoscope/Shutterstock.com; p. 17 Songquan Deng/Shutterstock.com; p. 19 wolf183/Shutterstock.com; p. 20 OakleyOriginals/Flickr; p. 21 Dan Kosmayer/Shutterstock.com; p. 22 David Unger/Shutterstock.com.

Library of Congress Cataloging-in-Publication Data

McAneney, Caitie, author.
 Look out for the raccoon! / Caitie McAneney.
    pages cm. — (Surprisingly scary!)
 Includes bibliographical references and index.
 ISBN 978-1-4994-0882-9 (pbk.)
 ISBN 978-1-4994-0905-5 (6 pack)
 ISBN 978-1-4994-0954-3 (library binding)
 1. Raccoon—Juvenile literature. I. Title. II. Series: Surprisingly scary!
 QL737.C26M424 2016
 599.76'32—dc23
                                    2015013146

Manufactured in the United States of America

CPSIA Compliance Information: Batch #WS15PK: For Further Information contact Rosen Publishing, New York, New York at 1-800-237-9932

CONTENTS

BACKYARD BANDITS

Have you ever seen a raccoon in your backyard? These ring-tailed **mammals** live almost everywhere in North America. They're often called "bandits" for the black masklike markings across their face.

Raccoons wander around neighborhoods, parks, forests, and cities, so they're common sights to see. They might look familiar, and even cute and cuddly, but these creatures can be harmful to humans. Raccoons can carry the rabies virus, which is very serious and can sometimes lead to death.

SKUNK

SURPRISINGLY TRUE!
Other animals that spread rabies include bats and skunks.

Rabies is a virus, or a small living thing that causes an illness. Rabies causes swelling in the brain of humans and animals.

WHERE DO RACCOONS LIVE?

The North American raccoon is found nearly anywhere from Central America to Canada. These raccoons have **adapted** to both **tropical** weather and cold weather. The North American raccoon is the most familiar species, or kind, and it's the species we'll focus on in this book.

Six other species of raccoons exist, but they mostly live on tropical islands. The crab-eating raccoon is a South American raccoon that lives as far south as Argentina. Raccoons have been brought to other parts of the world, such as Europe and Asia.

Raccoons have adaptations that allow them to live in certain weather conditions. The North American raccoon lives through the winter by becoming inactive and sleeping for long periods. This is a state called torpor.

RECOGNIZING RACCOONS

Raccoons are easily recognized because of their gray, white, and black markings. Their tails are ringed with black and white. They have white and black faces.

Raccoons grow to around 2 to 3 feet (61 to 91 cm). Their tail is about 1 foot (30 cm) long. Raccoons have four legs, and their back legs are longer than their front ones. Raccoons have five long toes on each of their front feet that can grasp objects. This helps them **forage** for food.

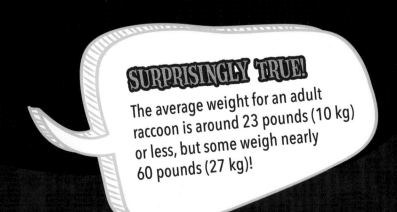

SURPRISINGLY TRUE!

The average weight for an adult raccoon is around 23 pounds (10 kg) or less, but some weigh nearly 60 pounds (27 kg)!

A raccoon's body might not look like it's built for movement, but raccoons are great at climbing trees, running, swimming, and jumping.

RACCOON BEHAVIOR

Raccoons are nocturnal, which means they're most active at night. You may see raccoons foraging and hunting if you're out at night. During the day, raccoons are resting in their dens. Raccoons make their dens in **burrows**, holes in trees and logs, and even in basements and attics.

Raccoons don't seem like very social animals. However, males and females do come together to mate, or make babies, between January and June. The babies, called kits, stay with their mother for about a year. The male doesn't help raise the kits.

SURPRISINGLY TRUE!

Scientists think raccoons are very smart. They can use tools and turn doorknobs. They're good at problem solving, such as overturning trash bins to get to the food inside.

Raccoons **communicate** with screams, whistles, hisses, and growls.

BOTH PREDATOR AND PREY

Raccoons use their quick, skillful paws for hunting **prey**. They often hunt around water because their paws can snag fish and frogs easily. They also grab eggs from nests and hunt bugs, squirrels, birds, and mice. Raccoons living near people eat out of trash cans, dog food bowls, and picnic areas.

Because raccoons hunt at night, they're safe from many daytime predators. Near cities and suburbs, there may be few predators. However, in the wild, raccoons are on the lookout for coyotes, bobcats, and cougars.

SURPRISINGLY TRUE!

Raccoons often put their food in water before eating it. Some people think they do this to wash the food, while others believe they're making their food softer to eat. No one is certain of the real reason!

Raccoons also eat plants and fruit. That makes them omnivores. They often sneak into gardens and farms for food.

THE PESKY RACCOON

When raccoons move into neighborhoods and cities, they can become quite a **nuisance**. They may try to make their homes under or around peoples' houses, causing harm to their property. They may even find a way inside a house. They're also known to tip trash cans over and make a mess!

Raccoons will usually hide or run away when they see a person. However, they've been known to sometimes attack people when they're scared. Raccoons sometimes bite, scratch, and even kill cats and dogs.

One way to keep raccoons away is to keep a tight lid on your trash can or keep trash cans inside.

SURPRISINGLY TRUE!

Leaving dog and cat food outside often **attracts** raccoons to your backyard.

Rabies is a disease, or illness, caused by a virus. This virus can be passed by touching the spit or brain matter of an animal with rabies. However, it's usually passed through a bite by a rabid animal.

The rabies virus enters the bloodstream through spit from the bite. Then, it attacks the **central nervous system**. Between two weeks and a year after the bite, a person may have a headache, sore throat, itching, and tiredness.

As rabies takes its course, a person will become paralyzed, or unable to move. They may die from a heart attack or inability to breathe. Luckily, rabies is treatable if it's caught early.

RABIES VIRUS

SURPRISINGLY TRUE!
Animals who get rabies may become **aggressive** or unafraid of people. They'll become unable to eat, drink, or walk straight. Finally, they'll become paralyzed and likely die.

IS THIS RACCOON RABID?

Not every raccoon has rabies. However, it's important to know the signs of rabies in animals.

A raccoon may have rabies if you see it outside in the daytime, instead of following its normal nocturnal behavior. It may be aggressive—biting, snapping, or growling at the air or at objects and animals around it. However, it may also look tired and tame. It may have a clumsy walk or seem partially paralyzed. It may have liquid coming out of its eyes or mouth. At this point, it will die within one to three days.

Seeing a raccoon during the day doesn't necessarily mean it has rabies. Many raccoons are active during the day, especially mothers with kits to feed. However, it's still important to stay far away.

RACCOON RISKS

There are many reasons to stay away from raccoons. While raccoons aren't usually aggressive, they're wild animals that sometimes lash out with their sharp teeth and claws. If a female is defending her babies, she may growl or try to fight a person or animal.

Raccoons also spread roundworm, which is a **parasite** that can infect people and animals. It's passed through eggs that end up in raccoon poop, or scat. When raccoons move into peoples' houses, they may leave scat that children or animals accidentally eat.

RACCOON SCAT

SURPRISINGLY TRUE!

If you've touched a raccoon or its waste and start to feel sick, go to a doctor right away!

Raccoons also spread a bacterial disease called leptospirosis. This possibly deadly disease may infect people who touch an infected raccoon or its waste.

21

SAFETY FIRST

It's important to be safe around all wild animals, but especially ones that carry diseases. Raccoons may look cute, but you should leave them alone. They usually don't want to fight. Never corner a raccoon. If they growl or arch their back, they're warning you. Walk away slowly. Bring in pets at night so they don't fight with raccoons.

It's possible for us to live peacefully with raccoons. Leave them alone, lock up food, and let them go on their way.

GLOSSARY

adapt: To change to fit new conditions.

aggressive: Showing a readiness to attack.

attract: To draw nearer.

burrow: A hole an animal digs in the ground for shelter.

central nervous system: A body system that includes the brain and spinal cord.

communicate: To share ideas and feelings through sounds and motions.

forage: To go from place to place looking for food.

hibernation: The act of spending winter in a deep sleep-like state.

mammal: A warm-blooded animal that has a backbone and hair, breathes air, and feeds milk to its young.

nuisance: A person, thing, or situation that causes trouble or annoyance.

parasite: A living thing that lives in, on, or with another living thing and often harms it.

prey: An animal hunted by other animals for food.

tropical: Warm and wet.

INDEX

WEBSITES

Due to the changing nature of Internet links, PowerKids Press has developed
an online list of websites related to the subject of this book. This site is updated
regularly. Please use this link to access the list: www.powerkidslinks.com/surp/rac